Dating Advice

The Ultimate Manual For Attracting Women: A
Comprehensive Handbook On Effortlessly Attracting
Women And Gaining Insight Into Female Psychology

*(Strategies For Achieving Your Desires And Discovering
Your Ideal Life Partner)*

Nicolas Hatfield

TABLE OF CONTENT

Handle Conflicts In a Healthy And Positive Way 1

Exercise Understanding And Empathy With Your Spouse.. 6

Proficiency in Communication 22

....39

Investigating Novel Aspects of Closeness 40

Engaging in Deeper Listening and Connection 67

Handling Rejection and Obstacles.................................90

Making Oneself Ready..123

Maintain Your Faith to Your Tastes............................145

Handle Conflicts In a Healthy And Positive Way

Any relationship will inevitably have conflicts, which are "vital," but how you handle them will determine how strong your bond is with your spouse.

It doesn't have to be harmful; rather, it should be a chance for you to get to know your partner better and develop as a couple. The secret is to resolve disagreements amicably and constructively instead of avoiding or intensifying them.

The following are some methods for settling disputes amicably and productively:

Select The Appropriate Time And Location. Don't start a conversation when you or your partner feel anxious, hungry, exhausted, angry, or preoccupied. Select a time and location where you may converse in privacy and without interruptions and when you are both at ease and relaxed.

2. Determine The Problem And The Objective. Make sure you both understand the nature of the problem and your goals for the discussion before you begin. Don't switch topics midway through or bring up too many topics simultaneously. Keep it to one problem at a time and find a solution that benefits you both.

3. Pay Attention and Show Empathy. Use the advice on effective listening from the first subject. Try to comprehend your

partner's perspective and feelings around the matter. Don't discount, condemn, or pass judgment on their viewpoint.

4. Use Clear and Respectful Expressions. Use the advice from the second topic to improve your communication skills. Talk about your thoughts and views on the matter. Furthermore, avoid blaming, attacking, or accusing your partner.

5. Try to Understand Rather Than Win. Refrain from viewing the disagreement as a contest or a game in which one of you must prevail while the other must fail. Instead, approach it as a partnership or cooperation in which you must cooperate to discover a solution that meets your requirements and desires.

6. Have An Open Mind To Negotiation And Compromise. Don't force your partner to agree or be stubborn about your beliefs. Be adaptable and receptive when settling on a compromise or a trade-off that benefits you both. For instance, you might say, "I'm willing to do this if you are willing to do that," and, "How about we try this for a while and see how it goes?"

7. Give An Apology And Let Go. Ask for forgiveness and provide an honest apology if you or your partner have erred or wounded each other's feelings. Similarly, show grace and generosity by forgiving and letting go of grudges and resentment. Never cling to the past or turn it against your spouse later on.

8. Look for points of agreement. Seek out areas of consensus and common objectives. This can assist you in cooperating to identify a compromise or resolution that meets the needs of both parties.

Steer clear of criticism and blame. Focus on communicating your wants and feelings to your partner rather than criticizing or accusing them of the argument.

Exercise Understanding And Empathy With Your Spouse

The capacity to place oneself in another person's position and experience their emotions is known as empathy. Understanding is The capacity to comprehend another person's ideas and intentions. You may strengthen your bond and mutual admiration by showing empathy and compassion for your spouse.

Here are some strategies for developing understanding and empathy:

● Show Interest and Curiosity. Inquire about your partner's interests, passions, dreams, goals, problems, anxieties, and other interests and hobbies.

- Offer Encouragement And Support. Congratulate your partner on all of their accomplishments, no matter how minor. Honor their accomplishments and encourage them. Tell them you believe in their potential and ability.
- Show kindness and compassion. When your partner feels down, hurt, angry, or anxious, comfort them. Express your condolences and support. Offer them a hug, a kiss, a grin, or encouraging words. Give them something kind or considerate.

- Show gratitude and respect. Even if your partner has different interests, views, boundaries, etc., than you, respect them nonetheless. Never try to sway them or make them live up to your expectations. Respect both your partner's virtues and shortcomings as well as their peculiarities. Don't ignore or undervalue them.

Effective communication is an essential ability that can improve any relationship, romantic or otherwise. You may enhance communication and build your relationship by learning to listen well, communicating honestly and openly, resolving disagreements healthily and productively, and showing respect and understanding for your spouse.

Remember that communication is something you should do daily, not just sometimes. It's a skill you develop via practice rather than something you pick up overnight. Furthermore, you work alongside your partner on it rather than by yourself.

Therefore, don't be scared to have informal or personal conversations with your loved one. Communicate with patience, kindness, honesty, love, respect, and humor. Learn to communicate with enthusiasm, curiosity, boldness, and joy.

Talk to your lover as though they were the most significant individual in the world.

Since they are!

How to Become a Beautiful Woman

To be considered beautiful, a lady needs more than a gorgeous body and a nice appearance. Some stunning women have no physical attractiveness at all. And then some unattractive women draw attention from guys no matter what. Each of us defines beauty in our unique way. Men, in particular, have different tastes in beauty. Continue reading to get quick tips on how to seem more appealing.

Be Your Person

Every one of us is special in our own right, as you well know. Focus on and develop your unique selling point to stand out. Women who stand out from the crowd attract the attention of males. Be unique. Please wear comfortable shoes and jeans instead of sexy, showy clothing if that is more your style.

Go ahead and choose to go shopping if you prefer riding horses. There's no point in following the herd since a woman who does so will never get any farther than the herd. However, a woman who travels alone discovers intriguing new locations that no one has ever gone to before.

Acknowledge and address your shortcomings. Highlight your positive traits and allow your true self to come through. You can never be more attractive with pretense.

Accept and Love Who You Are

Being who you are will be much easier if you love who you are. People pretend to be different because they find accepting who they are difficult. A gorgeous woman knows how to be confident in herself.

She treats her body with respect and cares for it. She recognizes her shortcomings but does not act self-conscious. She exudes confidence and doesn't hesitate to assert herself. A beautiful lady is content with who she is and is not readily swayed by the opinions of others about what is right or wrong.

Adhere to Your Principles

Men are always drawn to women who have strong moral convictions. It's critical that a woman pursues her goals and knows what she wants. Not knowing what she wants can be a little disheartening and annoying for a woman. The ability of a principled lady to uphold her moral values in the face of adversity is an alluring and lovely quality. Males look up to strong women.

Taking Care of Oneself

A lady who looks well looks after herself well. She has a healthy routine and lifestyle and is in good health. She spends her free time working out and occasionally getting her nails and hair done. She has a clean, fresh scent and is tidy. She consistently takes care of her skin and gets enough sleep. A beautiful woman maintains good hygiene yet doesn't mind becoming messy.

Being fit makes you feel good about yourself, which makes you glow from the inside out. It's seductive to be fit.

Sexiness equates to confidence, and confidence has a strong allure.

Grin

A woman with a cheerful attitude and a tendency to smile often is considered attractive. When a lady smiles, she looks her most gorgeous. A man's heart would melt from that alone. A woman gains more appeal in everyone's eyes if she is kind and personable. Similarly, a woman loses her beauty in the eyes of the public if she is unkind and difficult to approach. However, don't be so kind that you let other people walk all over you.

When the time comes, practice self-defense. Never make fun of other people. Refrain from being impolite and bullying others. When you have something to disagree with or are unhappy about, learn how to say it politely and calmly. Your calm and pleasant demeanor will quickly draw others to you. Avoid pretending to grin as well; it's impolite and frequently comes across as snarky.

Enjoy Life & Have Fun: A beautiful lady knows when to play it safe and when to take things seriously. She looks good when having fun and enjoying life with others. A lady who appreciates her life is content no matter her obstacles.

Be upbeat and focus on the positive.

Positive views on life and attitudes draw much attention from people of all genders. Unquestionably, a lady who never judges others and always shows compassion for them is highly appealing.

A beautiful woman is not one to be easily let down by life's events. Her belief that goodness exists in all people and circumstances sets her apart.

Step Outside

If you walk outside and enjoy the sun, people will only be able to recognize your attractiveness. You won't get noticed if you continue to hide. Take a whiff of the flowers outside. Grin and relish each moment of your existence. Joy has a contagious quality. It enhances a woman's natural beauty and attractiveness.

Communicate Yourself

A beautiful lady is aware of when and how to express herself. She has the intelligence to pick her words wisely and the courage to speak her mind. Though not scary, she is intelligent. She has a wide range of topics to discuss. She is not a dull companion and is very knowledgeable about her interests. Speaking your opinion and expressing how you feel are essential components of attractiveness.

Remain Resilient & Unwavering

A woman is undoubtedly exceptional if she perseveres in the face of many obstacles. A true woman goes after her aspirations and succeeds in them, even if it means making mistakes at first. Beautiful women are driven, prosperous, and self-assured.

Ultimately, the method you use to find a match is up to you. You may be more interested in quantity than quality, or vice versa. There are several methods for locating your ideal partner. Your dating site selection will limit the pool of potential matches, but your approach will cover the rest.

You can narrow down your search area and include a lot of criteria, which will provide you with a select group of highly qualified prospects.

Alternatively, you may choose to take the plunge. Some choose to speak with each match they receive to avoid dismissing possible mates for petty reasons. Your plan doesn't have to be determined from the start. You'll probably be too overwhelmed to figure out what suits you in the first place.

Getting What You Need From an Internet Conversation

This portion of the online dating experience is the same as the chat you would have if you ran into each other outside, even though you haven't met in person or at a bar. It takes one to initiate contact, and the opening statement should pique interest enough to sustain the exchange. Make it unique so that your match will remember you—after all, you are not their only match from today.

Although you can date in your jammies and converse with individuals from the comfort and safety of your home with online dating, you still need to abide by the standard conversational guidelines.

Words

Writing is currently your only means of communicating with the person you are attempting to get to know. Make sure to use whole phrases and proper English. Although emojis are personal, you shouldn't use too many of them.

Once more, compose a message as you would like to be read. Never use a cheesy or cheap pick-up line as a template. Don't start the conversation with sexual innuendos or remarks about their physical characteristics unless you are utilizing a website that is expressly and only focused on sex. Most people who take these sites seriously think it's tasteless, and they won't put up with it.

Make use of a reference from your match's profile if you can. Travels and music make excellent openers. Consider the information you included on your profile to draw interest. As you wrote about your favorite movies, your match has also mentioned things you enjoy doing in your own time.

Proficiency in Communication

In the dating scene, having good communication skills can help you forge meaningful relationships and handle difficult situations. This section will review important communication techniques to make dating more enjoyable.

4.1 Listening With Intent and Empathy

a. Active Listening: To practice active listening, give your date your whole focus. Refrain from being distracted by things like looking at your phone or planning your next sentence. You can indicate that you are paying attention by nodding, keeping eye contact, and making vocal cues like "I see" or "Tell me more."

b. Empathy: To better understand your date's perspective, imagine yourself in their shoes. Empathy fosters a closer relationship by expressing concern for their thoughts, emotions, and experiences.

c. Open-Ended Questions: Ask open-ended questions that demand a response beyond a simple "yes" or "no" to foster meaningful conversations. Asking, "What made your day remarkable?" is better than asking, "Did your day go well?"

d. Validate Feelings: Respect and give meaning to your date's feelings. "I understand why you'd feel that way," you're able to remark, or "It's perfectly normal to be nervous."

4.2 Establishing Boundaries and Being Assertive

a. Be Honest: Sincerity is essential when dating. Please express your emotions if you are not interested in pursuing a relationship. Being direct is better than leading someone astray.

b. Set Boundaries: Clearly define your dating boundaries. Inform us of the date of your willingness and lack thereof. Honor their boundaries as well.

d. Employ "I" expressions: When expressing your wants or feelings, use "I" statements to express yourself without criticizing or blaming others. Say, "I feel uncomfortable when..." rather than, "You make me uncomfortable when..."

d. Exercise Self-Advocacy: Speak out for your needs and wants courteously. In a partnership, expressing your needs and looking for win-win solutions is okay.

4.3 Making Compromises and Resolving Conflicts

a. Remain calm: Stay serene and cool during a conflict. Inhale deeply and make an effort not to worsen the circumstance.

b. Active Problem-Solving: See arguments as challenges that must be solved together. Recognize the issue, discuss potential fixes, and be prepared to make concessions.

b. Choose the Right Time: Timing is crucial when resolving conflicts.

Choose a convenient time and place for your conversation so that you and your date are ready to talk.

d. Give and take: Compromise is necessary for wholesome relationships. Ask your partner to make concessions and be prepared to give in on some matters. Establishing a happy medium is essential to the growth of relationships.

Good communication skills are essential to build relationships and resolve issues in the dating environment. You may create wholesome, polite relationships built on understanding and compromise using active listening, assertiveness, and conflict-resolution techniques.

Chapter 3: Capable Communication Techniques

Building genuine connections and dating successfully both depend on effective communication. You can communicate effectively, comprehend the viewpoints of others, and build sincere connections with great communication skills. Three key components of good communication—active listening and empathy, nonverbal cues, and conversational strategies—will be covered in this chapter.

Using Empathy and Active Listening

Paying close attention to and understanding what the other person is saying is active listening. It's important to comprehend what they say out loud and their motivations, feelings, and underlying message. Active listening fosters a stronger connection, affirms the other person's feelings, and demonstrates respect. Additionally, empathy plays a major role in good communication. Empathy promotes understanding and intimacy by enabling you to relate to and comprehend your dating partner's thoughts, feelings, and experiences. To display empathy and active listening abilities, act genuinely interested in the person, pose open-ended questions, and offer comments.

Nonverbal Interaction

Nonverbal cues frequently provide more information than just words. Understanding nonverbal cues can improve your ability to communicate with others and to understand yourself.

Among the most important elements of nonverbal communication are:

To project attention and confidence, keep your posture open and relaxed, create adequate eye contact, and employ movements that complement your speech.

The tone of Voice: Your intonation and tone greatly influence how people understand what you're saying. Effective communication of your intentions requires warmth, assurance, and clarity in your speech.

Closeness and Contact: Be aware of physical proximity and observe people's boundaries. Establishing rapport can be facilitated by appropriate touch, such as a warm embrace or a gentle handshake, but it's important to always get permission and respect each person's comfort zone.

Talking Points

It takes specific strategies that foster understanding and connection to have meaningful talks. The following are some techniques to improve your ability to converse:

Pose Inquiry-Based Questions: Asking open-ended questions invites the other person to elaborate on their experiences, hobbies, and self-disclosures. This demonstrates real inquiry and raises the conversation to a deeper level.

To show that you understand what the other person has said and that you are actively participating in the conversation, practice reflective listening by reflecting on what they have said. To build rapport, restate their arguments, acknowledge their emotions, and make encouraging remarks.

Tell Your Tales: Tell the other individual about your personal experiences and tales; this will inspire them to do the same. Telling one another's tales strengthens bonds, fosters trust, and enables more genuine communication.

Refrain from Interruptions and Engage in Practice Patience: Give the other person your attention and let them talk without interruption. As it demonstrates respect and interest, patience is essential to establishing connection and understanding.

In addition to honing your abilities, paying attention to and reacting appropriately to your date's cues and communication style is critical. By improving your communication skills, you may build a fulfilling and interesting dating experience that encourages meaningful relationships and understanding.

The upcoming chapter will discuss the value of creating an appealing lifestyle and how it can improve your dating chances.

Respect your appearance: Make time each morning to take a few moments to glance in the mirror and acknowledge your appearance. I adore everything about you—your face, body, hair, the color of your eyes, etc. You won't fall in love with every element of your body, but you should learn to accept the less attractive aspects of it. You can tell yourself, "I know my nose is too big, but I appreciate it because it ensures my breathing is effective," if your nose is too large. Anyone who truly loves you will find you attractive, but you must also acknowledge this to prevent insecurities from developing in a relationship.

Follow your enthusiasm:

Take up any activity that brings you joy. If swimming is the activity, begin swimming anytime you have free time.

If you enjoy hiking, look for hiking clubs and join them.

Engaging in activities you enjoy usually makes you happier and more appealing.

Being kind to yourself makes you feel lovely and joyful, which makes it simpler for you to tell men how great you are because you genuinely think it.

Step 3: Modify Your Perspective

Before beginning your love hunt, you must adjust your perspective and let go of the things that have kept you from finding love in the past. Your expectations are one of these things. When most of us search for a long-term spouse, we typically do so with preconceived notions about what an ideal mate should look like, what duties each partner should play, and how your partner should act.

Those expectations result in nearly every male you encounter feeling inadequate and let down. You should start evaluating guys based on your feelings for them rather than whether or not they meet your predetermined standards. This requires you to shift your perspective. Of course, there are reasonable expectations—I'm not talking about those—like wanting the person to be devoted, kind, and compassionate. I am referring to the expectation that you will desire a tall, attractive, filthy, rich man who will spoil you, take you out on dates, treat you like a queen, and so on. Since everyone has flaws, you must be open to accepting a man who is decent but not flawless.

Step 4: Clarify Your Goals

Usually, the pursuit of Mr. Right necessitates having a road map. To land your ideal partner, you must have a clear idea of the traits and expectations you have for him. You now need to decide what kind of man you want after having a mental shift.

You must consider the qualities you find most important and would like your new partner to have to accomplish that. Create a list of these items, then review it and mark the things you can and cannot compromise on. For instance, you might be drawn to a tall, dark, attractive Christian man who shows you respect and kindness. You can overlook that he is tall and black on that list in favor of him not being a kind and considerate Christian. You will have a distinct idea of what you truly desire in a man by the time you finish the list.

Following the above measures, you will be completely ready for a relationship. After getting ready, finding the greatest venues to hunt for a boyfriend is the next step.

➤ Meeting the Requirements of Each Partner

It's important to understand that everyone has varied levels of sexual wants and desires in a romantic relationship. A happy and successful sexual relationship depends on both parties understanding and respecting each other's preferences, boundaries, and wants.

Ensuring that each partner's sexual needs are satisfied enhances the feeling of equity and fulfillment in the partnership. It ensures that each person feels appreciated and loved, promoting a peaceful and well-balanced relationship. Although it is not the only factor that determines whether a relationship succeeds.

An essential component of a love relationship is sexual intimacy, which strengthens emotional ties, encourages intimacy and adds to happiness and contentment. It's a special and lovely method for couples to strengthen their love and understanding of one another by developing a physical and emotional connection. When it comes to sexual intimacy, it's critical to place a high value on open communication and mutual understanding to preserve a strong and healthy relationship.

Investigating Novel Aspects of Closeness

Over time, intimacy is a dynamic force that changes. Although the core elements of any relationship are physical, emotional, and sexual, many additional dimensions of intimacy can enhance and fortify the bonds between people.

1) Intellectual Closeness

The bond that develops between two people who exchange ideas, knowledge, and thoughts is known as intellectual intimacy. It's the flame that flares up in thought-provoking discussions and arguments. In addition to broadening their perspectives, couples who have thought-provoking conversations together develop a bond based on common values and worldviews. Intellectual intimacy encourages partners to push one another's viewpoints, grow intellectually, and learn from one another.

2) Close Spiritual Relationship

The bond created when people examine and discuss their values, beliefs, and life philosophies is known as spiritual closeness. It is not restricted to any particular religion; it can include a broad spectrum of spiritual or intellectual viewpoints. Engaging in spiritual conversations, rituals, or practices helps couples connect deeply because they desire to discover meaning, purpose, and connection in the cosmos. Spiritual closeness strengthens a relationship's sense of oneness and purpose.

3) Having Fun and Being Close

Sharing and taking pleasure in your partner's interests, pastimes, and travels is the essence of recreational intimacy. Cooking meals together, taking a walk, or engaging in a hobby like dancing or painting can all be examples. Enjoying leisure activities together as a couple deepens the relationship via humor, shared experiences, and the delight of making memories. Intimacy during leisure time inspires couples to appreciate each other's company and life.

4) Intimacy through Digital

The importance of digital intimacy has grown in the era of technology. It includes how partners interact and exchange information via social media, video calls, and texting. Even though you are physically apart, you can feel connected to your spouse even when you are not together by sharing your everyday activities, thoughts, and emotions with them online. It helps close the distance in long-distance relationships and preserve a feeling of unity.

5) Personal Experience

The core of experiential intimacy is relating special and unforgettable moments to your companion. TravelingSome examples are traveling to another nation, attending a performance, or attempting something new together, like skydiving or learning a new recipe. These joint experiences strengthen the emotional bond between couples and provide enduring memories. They serve as a gentle reminder to spouses of the life and excitement they each contribute to one another.

How to Increase Self-Assurance

Set and Meet Your Objectives

A fantastic strategy to boost confidence is to set and accomplish goals. Setting goals helps you achieve personal victories, which boosts your confidence. When you set objectives, you frequently break them down into smaller targets to meet along the way. A minor target would be five pounds, for instance, if your main objective was to lose thirty pounds. That's a victory, and your weight-loss journey gains confidence! This gives you more self-assurance and drive to keep going.

Take Chances

Taking risks is frightening and frequently requires facing fear, but the rewards are great. Let's say you have a fear of heights. Sitting near the top of the stands at a sporting event or strolling along the glass railing on the second or third floor of the mall could put you at risk.

Touching a snake or spider could be risky if you're terrified of them. Going to a pool with a very shallow end and gradually making your way into deeper water can conquer your phobia of the water.

You acquire confidence every time you confront a fear or take a chance. You discover that you have power over the anxiety you experienced due to your fear.

Act Morally

Whether you know it or not, you have a set of values that guide you in deciding what is good and wrong. The trick is that sometimes doing the right thing puts you in a difficult situation or requires more time than you would like to devote to it. Nevertheless, doing the right thing gives you a sense of satisfaction and increases your self-assurance.

We had an ice storm and snow a few years back. The parking lot was covered in ice while I was leaving the grocery store, so I had to carefully pay close attention to the ground to avoid slipping. For a split second, I looked up and saw an old woman trying to cross the parking lot. My goal suddenly changed, and I started walking towards her. I had to get to a job site quickly, but this was more important. How could that be my mother? I would want her to get assistance! Another man approached her and grabbed her arm before I could reach her. I was relieved she had arrived safely as he led her into the store.

I felt good about my willingness to help her, even if I couldn't get to her in time.

All I had to do was move away from the other guy. Her not falling was what mattered most.

Live a Fearless Life

We are afraid of failing. Fear is stigmatized, and no one wants to be associated with failure. However, what if you slightly alter the wording you use? Consider failure an opportunity to learn and improve rather than a bad thing.

Your fear of failing, not actual failure, is what keeps you disabled. Your fear of failing prevents you from taking those chances. It prevents you from exerting yourself a bit more than is perhaps comfortable. Nevertheless, you succeed when you overcome your fear, attempt something new, or step outside your comfort zone. Your resolve and self-assurance both increase.

Carry Out

Saying you'll walk 10,000 steps a day is simple, but it's simple to forget about it on day three when it starts to rain or you're exhausted. But it's a victory when you overcome your inner procrastination! You feel more self-assured and disciplined when you challenge the inner critic attempting to prevent you from improving. You've advanced each time you ignore your inner critic and keep going despite its advice to quit.

Establish a Workout Schedule

There are so many excuses we come up with not to work out. I injured my knee last week, and it might hurt again today. I'm too exhausted and busy; I'm also a little sore after yesterday's workout.

Exercise has so many positive effects on your bodily and emotional well-being that it would be difficult to list them here. Your endorphins will flow while you exercise, making you happy. lowers tension and anxiety, and benefits your heart.

You become more confident the more positive self-talk you have.

All of this is to argue that she's probably not flawless. And even though it can seem trivial, you ought to consider this the next time you approach a woman. She might be a nine to you. She may consider herself to be a 5. Everyone struggles with confidence, and very few genuinely believe they are flawless.

Furthermore, why would you want to date someone who believes they are flawless? This is significant because it reminds us that everyone has imperfections, even if we try to hide them from others. The dating world is no different. Therefore, don't feel terrible if you're pretending to be more confident than you are since, in the end, she most likely is too.

Having realized that women are human too and desire your attention, let's concentrate on getting you where you want to go: getting her to say yes.

Chapter 2: Reaching the Answer

Don't Allow Fear Prevent You From Reaching Out

Now that the game has begun. It's time to divide the boys from the men. You're prepared to apply all that you have discovered in the first section of this book. You're about to approach an extremely attractive girl you've set your sights on when suddenly. The next moment, your once-confident gait appears more like a limp. You're at a loss for words or actions. Do you think you should go up to her? Would you not want to?

You're staring at her across the room, your mind racing with many scenarios.

Perhaps she is already taken. Perhaps she is not fond of tall males. Perhaps she is not fond of short men. She's too excellent for you. It's too hot to get near her. You would never get her attention. You are going to make a fool of yourself.

You've been thinking about all those things before you approach her. Relax. As the well-known Disney film instructs us, sometimes you just have to let things go. Give over your uneasiness, trepidation, and fear. Alternatively, refrain from allowing it to control your behavior. Feelings are for losers; you do not need them. Alright. To be honest, you can't get too emotionally invested in a conversation with one random girl—perhaps that was too harsh.

You ought to be emotionally cold towards the circumstances. This meeting won't profoundly affect your life—unless you end up marrying her, but that's a story for another day. Therefore, you must not allow any of those unpleasant feelings to prevent you from approaching her. Every time you approach a female, you'll feel nervous, but you don't have to let it stop you from succeeding.

First of all, it doesn't matter if you're anxious. Act as though you aren't. Because you can tell yourself that you're confident and have this, to gain a yes is your aim. You don't have to analyze the situation—or, in this case, overanalyze it. It's not your job to devise a hundred reasons why she might say no to you. Little, your only priority at that point is to speak with her and persuade her to hear you out in less than thirty seconds.

This is neither a Toastmasters meeting nor a public speaking competition. You're just talking to a female, not participating in a live political debate. Remember this and simply act as though you are not anxious or tense. Once more, just push those unwanted—not to mention unjustified—emotions and feelings aside and take care of your business.

If you need to enroll in a few lessons to learn how to be more Zen, or if you need to start yoga to learn how to unwind, go for it. Take the necessary steps to overcome your self-doubt, which is mostly responsible for your anxiety, and to help you relax. You may even try approaching her after just inhaling deeply a few times. It's a traditional exercise that promotes physical and mental relaxation. Try to think optimistically if that doesn't work. Perform a few visualization exercises in which you picture yourself answering "yes." To make it happen, you need to visualize success. You're setting yourself up for failure if you're already visualizing failing. Recall that your goal is to initiate a conversation with a girl, not to complete an intense task like an untrained marathon. Consider approaching her as an opportunity rather than a challenge.

We've spent a lot of time discussing mindset adjustments, and the reason for this is that approaching a female will not always result in what you want it to. Many guys shy away from approaching girls out of fear of being evaluated by her and by random people who could overhear or are just passing by and going about their own business. They wish to avoid being made fun of. They wish to avoid humiliation. People generally desire to avoid placing themselves in any circumstance that could cause them even the slightest discomfort. Honestly, it makes sense—after all, who enjoys discomfort? As social beings, we naturally tend to care what other people think of us.

The good news is that you won't attract notice unless you're performing like a street performer or spinning on your head. Most self-assured people know that they are not the center of the universe. The distinction between individuals who are confident in themselves and those who aren't, even though this may seem paradoxical, is the understanding that not everyone is interested in them. As a result, they realize that nobody is deliberately criticizing them (well, not counting jealous jerks who use other people as a way to feel better). Being self-assured is simple when you understand that your image of yourself is the only one that counts.

How to Find Your Soulmate Online (Chapter 2)

What Draws Men to the Internet?

You'll need some advice on online dating for women if you will be effective at dating. Everything depends on first impressions. When finding a date, guys rely on their decisions on what you present on the first date. Men are unquestionably highly visual. Therefore, a lady will undoubtedly attract attention online with a strong photo. What do people search for, though, beyond the picture?

They do, after all, desire honesty in advertising. Men require reassurance that they will receive what they are seeking. You must display yourself rather than what you believe a guy would find attractive. Make every effort to portray yourself in your profile as someone they will meet on their first date if you're searching for a committed relationship. You will achieve more by doing this than acting like someone you are not.

It's better to portray yourself like you're conversing rather than merely listing your accomplishments and qualities like you're presenting a CV since men want to talk to people they believe to be real. They also want someone with whom they can go on adventures, so be sure to mention the kinds of physical activities you prefer in your profile. A man will be inspired to write once he sees that you share interests because he can immediately picture you enjoying your hobbies together!

Men dislike it when they see insecurity in a woman. Remember that they can tell if you're a needy person from a distance. Thus, you had best take action if you believe your self-esteem or confidence is lacking! But instead of writing about it, concentrate on the things you are confident about, like your job or sense of style. Confidence is attractive to men!

Men look for values in women as well. Women tend to back off when the topic of religion and family comes up because they fear coming across as overly serious and turning men off. This is untrue! Men who share your values will be receptive to your discussion of the truly important things to you!

When you build up your profile, keep the following points in mind: you will undoubtedly attract a lot of interest from males who could end up being your possible date!

Get Over Caring About What Others Think of You!

You will encounter positive and negative outcomes as you put the knowledge from the book into practice. Effectively navigating the rollercoaster of diverse experiences and learning to be successful with women can be likened to mental training. You become stronger mentally as a result of this. Therefore, You may consider that in your pursuit of success with women, you will experience so much shaking, fiddling, and shock that your brain will genuinely strengthen like a muscle. This chapter will discuss how to emerge from these situations as a boss.

feeblemindset

Avoid being the man who approaches a female, attempts to make a move, and then makes a huge issue out of it, saying things like, "Did you see that that girl liked me? I'm so cool; I'm a pimp?" and talking about it for weeks afterward. When things don't work out, they physically repeat the incident in their minds like a mental movie, attempting to come up with an excuse, piece together this shaky narrative of who they are, and convince themselves that it doesn't matter that this happened.

To succeed with women, you must have a strong mental muscle that allows you to process and swiftly notice offenses to your reputation or self-image.

We divided it into five categories because it's a mental muscle developed by success with women. These five mental taxonomy-inducing activities strengthen your brain like a muscle, enabling you to withstand more negative stimuli without losing your strength.

These five items consist of:

- Excessive stimulation
- Circumstances with High Social Pressure
- Refusals

- Unfavourable Evenings

"One-It-Is"

Overstimulating Circumstances

You'll quickly encounter this if you go out in upscale settings, such as nightclubs. It can be challenging if you're a guy who has never been to a club. Rather than persevering and gradually becoming desensitized to it, most people simply leave that area. People also go through this at different points in their journey when they go to a first-rate, grotty nightclub. It's overwhelming; sometimes, they can't even think, and it seems like their mind shuts off, and they don't even remember their night. Eventually, they get used to it and move on to better and better clubs. Places you don't feel deserving of being.

This is what it takes to succeed with women. One thing that helps build mental toughness is forcing oneself to venture out into slightly more affluent settings because that's where the attractive women hang out, instead of simply sticking in places where you're comfortable. It will slightly alter your mental state, but the effects of constantly being thrust into unfamiliar situations are astounding.

Be joyful even if it's frightening. Occasionally, guys say things like, "It's a scary environment, it's hectic, there's a lot of competition, there's loud music," when they hear the phrase "go to nightclubs." Take pleasure in that. Going out during the day or to a pub is a joke in comparison if you become numb to that. You improve on a more challenging playground. Accept it and make an effort to seek out these unpleasant situations.

Engaging in Deeper Listening and Connection

Section 1: What Active Listening Is All About

Anna understood that giving someone your whole attention extended to deeper levels of social interaction in the sleepy town of Congruity Safe House. She realized that the key to fostering meaningful friendships was listening to and comprehending what others were saying.

Anna learned to be mindfully present during conversations by paying close attention to the speaker. She believed focusing on the moment and avoiding distractions were necessary for receiving complete attention.

Nonverbal Cues: Anna recognized that nonverbal cues such as making eye contact, gesturing, and communicating openly conveyed her genuine interest and desire to participate in the conversation.

Section 2: Establishing Emotional Bonds

Empathetic Understanding: To truly understand the speaker's feelings and points of view, Anna practiced sympathetic tuning in by putting herself in their shoes. This grabbing extends deep connections.

Asking Thoughtful Questions: Anna encouraged the speaker to delve further into their experiences and points of view by asking subtle but perceptive questions. This training sparked important discussions.

Section 3: Encouraging Vulnerability and Trust

Validation and Acceptance: Anna created a safe space for the speakers to express themselves honestly by endorsing their feelings and interactions. She realized that acceptance and recognition fostered vulnerability and created trust.

Sharing in Return: In response to her frailty, Anna shared her reflections and experiences. She thought that common sharing was a fair and legitimate exchange.

Tasks and Thoughts:

Exercise Being Aware: Take part in a conversation and emphasize being fully present. Consider the implications of this presence on your interpretation of the conversation.

Practice Empathetic Listening:

Pay attention to a friend's or a family member's narrative.

Try to put yourself in their shoes and comprehend their thoughts, feelings, and experiences.

Recall the insights that have been recently uncovered.

Pose Unrestricted Questions: Select an interesting topic and engage in a dialogue where you ask open-ended questions to encourage more discussion.

Important lessons learned:

Being Aware: During conversations, give your full attention while avoiding interruptions and demonstrating genuine interest.

Empathetic Understanding: To truly understand the speaker's feelings and points of view, practice sympathetic listening.

Validation and Sharing: To create meaningful connections and foster trust, validate feelings, ask perceptive questions, and address vulnerability.

Giving someone your whole attention allows you to connect with them more deeply and establish relationships based on understanding, compassion, and respect. It's a revolutionary tool. This part emphasizes how important it is to be accessible, practice understanding with compassion, and foster a safe and transparent environment for certified associations.

Keep Yourself Alive

People frequently change into the type of companion that their spouse desires. While this is positive, one can only take things so far. It's possible to lose oneself when one tries too hard to impress others.

This train does not have a promising future. One of the spouses will eventually resent the other because they believe they are being usurped.

Avoid Combining Signals

This is reciprocal. Avoid giving conflicting messages to the other person and avoid reading nonexistent signals. Everyone is extremely busy these days, and nobody has time to play video games all day.

Send out only the meant signals; when things don't work out, be prepared to accept them. It is important to keep in mind that this is a two-person game.

What if it doesn't end up working out?

Holding yourself responsible for the entire situation is never really the best idea. Move forward and take lessons from the past.

Modern dating and mating are far easier these days. You only need direction, a strong sense of adventure, and clarity.

9. Advice For Creating A Lasting Relationship

Women desire to meet someone they can call their real love. One of the main motivations for people in the dating environment is this. Even while dating can be exhilarating in this day and age of advanced technology, these relationships frequently do not last very long.

Currently, 50% of marriages in the United States alone terminate in divorce. It would appear that developing a strong relationship is harder than one might imagine. But, this does not imply that all is lost or hopeless—just because half of marriages terminate in divorce.

Some unions survive and continue to be lifelong commitments that offer their members unconditional love and happiness in addition to immense delight and calm. How exactly can one accomplish this?

There are certain common actions that one can do. These important actions will help you set up your relationship for success. Among them are:

Developing a Trusting Relationship It is common for relationships to face difficulties when two people become attracted to one another. Despite the widespread belief that love is unbreakable, there are some obstacles that even the closest relationship cannot overcome if they are not addressed correctly.

Trust is one such difficulty. There is no chance for a union to last if one does not have total faith in their spouse. One of the most basic needs in a relationship is complete trust. To know that one partner always has the best interests of the other in mind, one must know them well enough. They must also be able to put their faith in one another to maintain the integrity of their connection.

Love Without Conditions

A lot of people view relationships as stepping stones to something greater. As a first step towards: * A better financial situation; * A better social standing (trophy spouses); * A debt relief strategy; * A cover-up for something else (gays marrying heterosexuals to avoid stigma)

All relationships have a purpose, but one of the most important ones is the inclusion of unconditional love. The partnership won't endure without total devotion and love between the partners. There will eventually be disdain.

Respect for One Another

The days of seeing one partner in a partnership as a lesser shareholder are long gone. Women today earn just as much as males, if not more, and there is no restriction on how they can communicate.

There won't be respect or acknowledgment between union members until they are mutually contemptuous. Having open lines of communication with one another will strengthen your relationship. Supporting one another through this communication is also very important. A connection is meaningless and lost if it doesn't aim to improve itself.

When developing a relationship, the final result is the joint responsibility of both sides. Both parties are responsible for articulating their goals for the partnership and identifying a common ground from which to build each other's aspirations.

It was never Facebook's intention to facilitate blind dates. The only individuals you should connect with are those you already know. Adding random strangers to your friends list on purpose is against their guidelines. Furthermore, most of the girls on Facebook aren't there to date. Because of this, you shouldn't often expect to start flirting with them at random and have favorable answers unless you use certain strategies, which I'll review in the following pages. First of all, you must realize that Facebook and "dating websites" are not the same. It entails attempting to meet women on Facebook using the same strategy on a dating website like Match.com, where users are there primarily to find love or casual relationships.

The desires of women

You have to know what women desire from you before you can start changing your Facebook profile. The idea that women aren't motivated by reason is the most fundamental one in female psychology. For them, emotion is everything. It all comes down to how a guy makes her feel in her stomach, and this same broad idea applies to digital seduction. This is why they become agitated and often even upset over things that appear absurd to us. However, if you know how to arouse specific feelings in them, you can take advantage of women's emotional nature. Why do nice girls go out with "bad boys"? Because girls who are attracted to terrible boys experience intense emotions. Although there could be continual turmoil in their relationship, and he may mistreat and cheat on her, women become addicted to the emotional roller coaster that terrible boys provide. The fact that terrible lads don't need anything is one of the main reasons they appeal to women like crack cocaine. They are self-reliant, go their way, and attract the attention of other women, which makes the women they are with want to cling to them even more.

Remember these attributes. When interacting with women on Facebook, you should project them to them. Additionally, you can transmit these traits subtly; it's not necessary to appear arrogant or like a "tough guy." It's about showcasing your differences from most guys. You're not needy or needy-bearish. You're a guy who enjoys a great, exciting lifestyle. Your alternatives are virtually limitless. However, the invitation is open for her to board your train and experience the ride of her life. You can't fail when this is reflected in how you present yourself on Facebook.

As you are undoubtedly aware, if you regularly read my books and subscribe to my VIP email, I adore the idea of High-Status behavior. There's one more thing you should know about this. Compared to men, women are far more concerned with their social standing. They are extremely sensitive to what their friends and peers think of them. Additionally, they're constantly looking for methods to rise in their peer group's social hierarchy.

For this reason, women tend to use Facebook far more than males. Compared to us, they update significantly more regularly. Additionally, they secretly yearn for "likes" and comments on their updates since it helps them feel validated. For a woman, nothing matters more than her social standing. They value it far more than having sex.

Setting Off Social Proof

This is essential to your Facebook success. Maybe the best method to persuade people—not just girls—is through social proof. Reviews and testimonials are crucial for your items because of this. How can you make girls feel that way?

The stunning ladies who are either their friends or lovers provide guys who are successful with women with social proof. This is represented on Facebook by the users commenting on your posts, friends list, and images. It presents you as a man women can trust and should get to know when they see you interacting positively and receiving great feedback from other women. Preselection is the most effective method for igniting a strong and instantaneous attraction on Facebook and in real life. Other women will notice if attractive ladies are all about you and enjoying your company. They will conclude that you are a dominant figure in society.

Indeed, there are occasions when you have to pretend to be successful (after all, everyone starts someplace). Furthermore, using your profile, it's far simpler to "fake" it on Facebook. Eventually, though, you have to be the

REAL THING and the personification of the person your profile portrays.

Sustaining an Upbeat Attitude and Vitality

For older guys, dating might be a scary idea. You are looking to start again after having your fair share of experiences. It's common to feel a little nervous when meeting someone for the first time in person, but it's crucial to keep your spirits up. Maintaining your positivity and receptivity will help you make a favorable impression.

Being self-assured is the first step in keeping a happy attitude. While some nervousness is normal, it's crucial to remember that you have a lot to contribute. Be proud of your identity and emphasize your positive traits since confidence is attractive. Let your self-belief and ability to succeed serve as the cornerstones of your mindset.

Being receptive to new experiences is another strategy for keeping a pleasant outlook while meeting someone in person. Don't stress over attempting to impress the other individual with your expertise or background. Rather, concentrate on getting to know them better and being receptive to any experiences they might have to offer.

Maintaining your enthusiasm and energy is also crucial. Your attitude and energy level may indicate you feel exhausted or depressed. Make sure you receive enough rest and that you take breaks as needed. Enjoy stimulating and energizing activities, including walking or listening to music.

Lastly, work on your communication abilities. Paying attention to what you say and how you carry yourself is critical. Talk clearly, and pay attention. Show consideration and refrain from passing judgment or being critical. This will assist you in establishing a welcoming environment where you may both feel free to express yourselves.

These are just a few pointers for keeping your spirits and attitude pleasant while meeting someone in person. Recall that dating may be enjoyable and fulfilling. You will make a lasting impression with the correct mindset and enthusiasm.

Handling Rejection and Obstacles

setbacks when meeting individuals in person, particularly for older guys reentering dating. The thought of being rejected or dealing with a setback might be frightening.

But if you approach these obstacles with the correct mindset, you can overcome them and emerge stronger and more self-assured.

Above all, it's critical to acknowledge that rejection and disappointments are inevitable. They are something that everyone goes through at some point, and they may be a tool for growth and development. Feeling angry or sad when you're rejected or have a setback is normal. However, try to accept it and utilize it as a chance to think about who you are and how you date.

Rejection and setbacks are best dealt with by maintaining a good attitude. Remain detached from the situation and avoid taking it too seriously. Recall that it's merely a signal that you might need to modify your strategy or try something else, not a reflection of who you are.

It's critical to stay focused on your objectives. Rejection and disappointments don't have to be the end of your dating life. Improve yourself, focus on your controllable circumstances, and confirm that you are progressing toward your goals.

Surrounding oneself with a network of friends and relatives who can validate and support you can also be beneficial. It might also be good to talk to people who have gone through similar experiences since they could have useful tips or coping mechanisms for handling rejection and failures.

Lastly, don't be afraid to take chances and try new things. The more you put yourself out there, the greater your chances of success. Accept rejection and setbacks as part of opening yourself up to new experiences and measured risks.

When meeting people in person, it can be difficult to navigate rejection and setbacks. Still, it's crucial to remember that you can use them as opportunities to improve yourself. Remain upbeat, committed to your objectives, and unafraid to take chances. You can overcome these obstacles if you have the correct mindset and strategy.

Finding the most important personality features

When establishing a close relationship with a woman based on intimacy, it is helpful to have the correct attributes, such as kindness, empathy, affection, and a desire to provide and receive emotional support. You can determine whether a woman possesses these qualities by examining her actions toward you. Does she like to touch, hug, or kiss you? Does she care about your hobbies, prior experiences, and social life? You may ask her outright what she thinks is important in male-female relationships.

But it's crucial to delve further. To win a man over, a woman may first treat him better than her actual conduct shows. As such, be mindful of oblique cues. Examine how she interacts with people and the environment in various settings, including how she engages with customers, coworkers, friends, parents, strangers on the street, etc. And pay attention to what she says about these individuals. If it looks right, learn more about her past relationships—what she liked and didn't enjoy, how they were formed, what she thinks of her ex-partners and why.

Locating a woman who shares your interests

Spending quality time together is one of the most important factors for developing a good personal relationship. You must have endless conversations on subjects that both of you find fascinating and significant. Having similar interests in books, music, movies, TV series, extreme sports, fitness, and traveling is also beneficial. You can search locations where like-minded individuals congregate, such as social media communities, interest clubs, and themed events, to locate a woman who shares your interests. You can also examine her social media presence to learn more about a woman's interests, writing style, uploaded images, and accounts she follows.

2.2. ardor

Sex attraction is the basis for this group of demands. It covers every necessity about strong emotions, such as drama, romance, flirtation, and sex. If your main need is passion, find a lady who is not actively seeking emotional intimacy or a committed relationship but who shares your desire for strong feelings. Knowing what to search for can make it simple to find such a woman. A lady who displays her sexuality in public, whether through provocative tweets or acts, enticing gazes, or revealing attire, is probably a brilliant individual and could make a wonderful match. It's crucial to distinguish between people who truly seek out emotional encounters and those who flaunt their sexuality for commercial gain.

Because they are afraid of being judged or have low self-esteem, most women who crave sex and strong experiences may not publicly express it. The most important thing when choosing a lady who is right for you is whether or not she has expressed a desire for intimacy and a relationship through her actions and talks. Women who are seeking meaningful relationships and emotional closeness should be avoided because it is unfair to mislead them into believing that you share their desires. This kind of activity is deemed immoral in our view.

Rather, give time to locate a woman who shares your interests. Society used to dictate that it was disgraceful for women to look for a spouse solely for sex. But attitudes about partnerships are shifting, and women are becoming more honest about their needs and wants.

The to-do list for your next big thing

A few years ago, I recalled being tired of all the bubbly city girls and realizing I needed to find a meaningful relationship. I belonged to a group of girls who felt it was time to make the most of our lives.

My friend Alisha invited us for a girls' night out and said she had a solution to help us get along.

"Now is the perfect time to get to know our future selves."

She then gave some sheets to each of us.

For all of us, the sheets were a complete revelation. In addition to being enjoyable, the exercise gave us a foundation for what we would need to attract our ideal partners.

I want to share the same concept with you today because it will benefit me.

Using a pen and paper, make a note of the selections you made from the list below:

✓ Relationship title: Alright, so we've previously talked about this. So, decide what to do. Is it a financial sponsor, FWB, fuck buddy, or fiancé?

✏ Where does your partner live? Does proximity truly matter, or is it not a big deal?

✏ connection duration: Ask yourself if you need a long-term friend, a casual connection, or a contract partner.

✏ Ideal age: Write it down.

✢ Essential prerequisites: Enumerate five attributes that your potential partner must possess to be considered for the partnership, such as being clever, having a common outlook on life, being financially stable and independent, and having solid life skills.

✏ Qualities of interest: List five qualities, such as a love of children, physical attractiveness, trustworthiness, shared interests, and strong leadership abilities, that you would be happy to see in a candidate.

✐ Flexibility areas: Since no candidate can be flawless, name five vices you can live with (though some might consider them deal-breakers), such as drinking, smoking, race, religion, sense of style, and personal hygiene.

✐ Deal breakers: List the top five characteristics, such as being disrespectful, selfish, diet-obsessed, pessimistic, nagging, etc., that you would never be able to put up with.

✐Your benefits: How will forming a relationship with you help the chosen candidate? List the things you will be contributing to the discussion. Characteristics like being a great kisser, easygoing, clever, sensitive, kind, and honest make you a jackpot and a once-in-a-lifetime opportunity.

Why does this approach work so well?

Using the checklist, you may easily verify who is eligible, who isn't, and who would seem to fit in well with your life. It's a fantastic technique to employ at different points in your life when you can be searching for a life partner, mentor, friend with benefits, fuck buddy, or sponsor. It will be harder for you to focus on time wasters if you are certain and clear about the traits of the ideal applicants.

It is important to note that most individuals in the romantic realm choose long-term partnerships over short-term agreements and engagements. You really ought to be ready for this.

This indicates avoiding forming connections based on availability, closeness, and mutual loneliness. The relationship is doomed if you do.

Similar to my friend Carolina, who turned the family electrician into a fuck buddy, she ultimately became an unhappy person.

So, how do you separate the rascals from the virtuous ones?

It's not as simple as you might assume, but be cautious around bad lads since they have warning signs. For example, I've discovered that manipulators frequently communicate excessively, especially through text messages.

However, great guys are also truly occupied and genuinely communicate with each other. This guy will pick up the phone to give you a precious, unbroken session and will dedicate his time to doing so. The exceptional man respects your time and won't make you adopt a trait. Seldom will he change arrangements, call impromptu meetings, or cancel dates. He respects your timetable and knows it is just as valuable as his. The bad lad, as you might expect, is the complete opposite.

You should make other guys you meet follow this practice as a high-value lady. Losers typically write themselves off since they are unable to follow your rules. They'll even refer to you as manipulative and arrogant. Interestingly, excellent men will follow your guidelines and only voice mature objections when necessary.

There are a ton of different strategies that we should explore immediately to prevent falling for the bad boys.

Initial Thoughts

One of the book's most underappreciated yet powerful strategies is making an entrance. It enhances the likelihood of drawing even more people to flirt with you and allows everyone on the lookout to see you at your finest rather than having you do all the running.

Stars turn heads when they walk on stage because they want to draw attention to themselves and their surroundings. Making a spectacular entrance causes others to sit up and take notice, as well as capturing the interest of the person you wish to impress. An entrance can be used to get both professional and excellent flirting outcomes. Make the most of every opportunity to make an impressive entrance, as it will impress clients and colleagues. Your main goal is to stand out from the crowd as soon as you enter a room.

Creating a memorable first impression is one of the simplest methods to attract attention. Every time you enter, become familiar with and put these into practice:

- Pause at the beginning of each entrance. Entering a room abruptly or clumsily is not elegant.
- Take advantage of the pause to stand up straight, push your shoulders back, tuck your chest in, keep your tummy in, raise your head, and stare straight ahead.
- Even if you are alone, turn to face the most crowded area of the room and smile. When you smile, people regard you as a friendly, well-liked person and keep thinking about you throughout the evening as someone worth speaking with.

- To give those looking the best chance to accept you, move slowly but statuesquely toward the busiest area of the room.
- Look people in the eye while you survey the space. Those who are interested or available are the ones you will notice are the ones who are observing.

If Brad Pitt and Angelina Jolie walked the red carpet like Homer and Marge Simpson, would the paparazzi be after them? Unlikely. A deviation from the usual in body language attracts attention. For instance, firm, confident motions attract attention from others and have aphrodisiac properties. People who walk differently due to a disability, for example, or who have clear body language and distinctive movements, stand out.

If you flip through a magazine, you'll notice that celebrities all have the same facial expressions. These folks are never slouching or lowering their heads unless they're embarrassed or catch the paparazzi off guard. Use the following star-like body language:

• Maintain an elongated neck and forward-facing gaze while holding your head high. This posture exudes power, sexiness, and control.

• Maintain a backward posture with your shoulders thrown back and your chest bared: You're beckoning folks to approach you by doing so. People gravitate toward you like your chest is a fisherman's line.

A slow, steady scan of the room shows that you're self-assured and composed enough to stand motionless and observe your surroundings before deciding which person or group to join. Don't avert your sight from making eye contact.

Consider stairs as an excellent chance to outshine everyone else in the room rather than just a means of transportation from one place to another.

- To help you maintain your balance, hold your position before moving forward. Women wearing high heels should pay particular attention to this delay.
- To guarantee a smooth fall, measure the space between the stairs.
- Step on your toes.
- When descending, keep your head up and avoid looking down. Your peripheral vision is essential for staying aware of your surroundings, judging what's underfoot, and spotting potential dangers like carpets, slick floors, uneven stairs, etc.

Your stunning body language draws attention, but if you place yourself strategically, the impression is amplified, and you become a magnet for individuals hoping to flirt.

Big-time stars purposefully place themselves in the greatest positions to showcase their best qualities and provide excellent viewing possibilities for everyone, rather than lurking around the edges or hiding behind pillars. There's a solid reason actors typically vie for the front of the stage; it gets them the greatest attention and spotlight. You must take up the proper position in the room to interact with the most individuals possible.

A place where you can see what's happening and where the greatest number of people can see you well is called a power spot.

In a corporate setting, the most dangerous position is directly behind the door with your back to it; the best seat in the room is the one furthest from the door and has the best view of it. Research indicates that individuals seated opposite doors in business meetings, offices, or restaurants experience increased heart rate and consequent anxiety compared to those facing the door.

Single people in bars and clubs keep one eye on the entrance and the other on the restroom since these areas have the most activity and allow them to observe people in motion without feeling like they are being observed. Stairs that stand out between levels are also interesting to see.

Paying attention to the door is a rudimentary safety measure. The cavemen sat facing the entrance and fire, their backs to the wall, watching for potential threats. While we no longer worry about being ambushed by a saber-toothed tiger, we pay attention to who enters and leaves a room.

You've mastered your star moves and identified the room's hotspots. Then all you'd have to do is wait for someone to notice you. You can, however, take the lead and initiate contact if you want your flirting success rate to be higher. Not only will the other person feel flattered that you've approached them, but you'll also be in charge of the situation and making the decisions rather than waiting for the other person to take action before the chance passes.

Individuals tend to fret excessively about what they would say to break the ice during a flirtation. They try to think of complex or witty starting statements to make themselves seem more fascinating. Making the initial move in a flirtation can be the most nerve-wracking because it puts you in danger of being rejected or looking foolish. You can reduce this danger, though.

Guys, words have so much power!
You can try an amazing "trick" by beginning the sentence with "my friend" or "this guy." This has crazy amounts of power in it. At that point, you are free to say anything you wish. This takes accountability for your words right away, thus granting you unrestricted speech. You might still arouse those sexual feelings at the same moment.
Oh, and the greatest part is that many girls may question if the person they call

their friend is you in the back of their minds when they hear the phrase "my friend." It's positive because she will probably take more time to consider whether you are truly not the person you claim to be unless you specifically name your friend.

Here's an illustration:

"Hey, I have a question for you regarding my friend. He is very fond of giving neck kisses, thanks to Instagram. He claimed that girls adore it.

"I kind of wanted to tell you about something my friend told me, but I'm not sure if you can handle it," he said.

Her: "It's what? I think I can handle it.

Him: "He mentioned that the woman he is seeing wanted him to act out the scenario from Fifty Shades of Grey. The part when he gives her a kiss after we finish the wine and the part where he uses his mouth to massage an ice cube along her body while she is wearing a blindfold. Does he have to do it?"

Idea #2: Develop Her Subconscious Mind
Here's where we can tease her with words to persuade her to consider sexuality.

For instance, if you were sharing a chapstick or coffee cup with a girl.

"There's no hiding it," you say.

Her: "How come?"

"I know you raped your chap stick when you got home," said you.

"I understand that my lips are flawless and soft, but please give that cheap vitamin E tube a break," you tell them.

I put "soft and perfect" in bold because those will make her think about your lips without realizing it, and you know what happens when a female thinks about lips. She's thinking about kissing you, not about cutting the lawn!

Okay. We live in a wonderful time where you can practice this stuff with random girls you have never met and probably never will meet on Twitter/Instagram and Tinder. If you haven't already, it's time to TAKE ACTION.

You'll discover how to adjust your texting style to suit your individuality. I am aware that some of you reading this are trying to get better at texting to help you get that one girl. Or perhaps all you want is a girlfriend. However, you must be texting other women if you aren't in a committed relationship.

It will greatly improve your social abilities, help you make friends, boost your confidence, and win your respect. Remember that a woman believes you to be a high-profile person if you have been "pre-approved" by other women.

You'll be forced to step outside of your comfort zone by this, and that's when change happens. Set a goal to obtain "x" numbers in "x" time. A newbie should aim for ten consistent numbers in 14 days. Additionally, restrict your intake to only 3–4 via internet sources.

Double dates are typically between close friends. This is quite convenient because your best buddy gets to meet your date and vice versa. Additionally, you become more relaxed and organic. However, you do not want to have conflicting personalities, so make sure that everyone at the table can get along with one another. You and your date don't get along well with it. Furthermore, your friend and their date may ruin your date—not because of anything you did. That is even more melancholy and unpleasant, so be cautious about that.

Selecting the appropriate dating style and setting clear expectations can undoubtedly assist you in meeting the "right one." Doing so can maximize your positive traits and reduce any negative ones. If you carefully study these suggestions and remember that the most successful dates are those you plan for, you will undoubtedly find your ideal match.

Making Oneself Ready

With that knowledge, you will undoubtedly be better able to prepare for your date. Regardless of the date type—casual, double, blind, or otherwise—it is essential to know what and how to prepare. You do not want to appear awkwardly attired, with excessive makeup, or even appear foolish because you did not give your date a single thought. That is undoubtedly the last thing you wish to convey to that individual. Therefore, what better way to avert this catastrophe than preparing yourself for that date?

Regardless of your gender, achieving an appropriate atmosphere is the primary requirement before embarking on a romantic outing. Your disposition will undoubtedly determine the course of the remainder of the evening. Remember that just as your date expects you to have a good time, he or she does the same. Therefore, to facilitate the experience for both of you, ensure that your mood is exceptionally upbeat to make your date more enjoyable and less monotonous.

Additionally, you must ensure that you are well-rested before the date, as most of them occur after dinner. This indicates that both of you have completed your tasks and obligations for the day before your date. Both of you, or perhaps just one of you, may be exhausted from the day's work-related obligations and the strain of the workplace. A short power nap is the most effective way to ensure you are well-rested for that date. Napping for no longer than thirty minutes is sufficient. It is crucial that you, at the very least, have the opportunity to unwind for a brief period to clear your mind and improve your mood. This will assist you in maintaining an optimal level of vitality for your date.

If possible, an additional piece of advice to help you attain the ideal disposition and vitality for that date is to shower. Showering may serve as a method of relieving tension for certain individuals. It stimulates relaxation not only in the psyche but also throughout the body. This will assist in alleviating any muscle tension that your date may be experiencing. Additionally, it will enhance your appearance for the upcoming date. Additional points have been awarded to you.

Additionally, exuding a delightful aroma will assist you in slaying that date night and ensuring its success. A deliberate effort to allure your date by emitting a pleasant scent is crucial, as it will affect your experiences together. The influence of fragrance can be quite deceiving. However, when utilized appropriately, this will undoubtedly elicit admiration from your companion regarding the actions you took while emanating that scent. It resembles personal branding through a fragrance. Furthermore, what better way to leave a lasting impression than through your fragrance?

Before your date, organize your attire to prevent yourself from panicking and appearing like a wreck. Additionally, you do not wish to impart this perception to your companion. Therefore, do not feel culpable if you meticulously consider the attire you intend to wear on your date. It does not indicate that you are frantic or dependent on using that date. However, considering your attire will ensure your date is a tremendous success.

For a casual look, gentlemen should don button-down polo shirts and trousers. It is highly inappropriate to wear shorts and an ordinary T-shirt; doing so would give the impression that you have just returned home. One desires to appear both attractive and adorable. Constantly wear closed footwear, such as trainers or leather shoes, for a more professional appearance.

Girls should accessorize casually by donning simple dresses or adorable skirts complemented by fashionable blouses. Extremely short skirts and short shorts should be avoided to prevent one from appearing to be a slut seeking someone to flirt and sleep with. Embrace the occasion by donning heels, or opt for the more comfortable alternatives of flats or sandals. Never wear flip-flops on a date; doing so would completely spoil the occasion.

Ingenious Date Concepts

The initial phases of a new relationship are enchanting and filled with anticipation. To foster a more profound emotional bond and establish enduring recollections, deviating from the norm and injecting originality and creativity into your encounters is critical. This guide aims to assist you in generating original and creative date concepts that will foster a stronger bond between you and create a lasting impression of your time together.

Artistic Expeditions: Engage in collaborative exploration of artistic endeavors to unlock your creativity. Engage in a pottery or painting course, visit a nearby art gallery, or dedicate an afternoon to crafting your works of art. Through the distinct means of bonding that artistic expression provides, it fosters a deeper connection among participants.

Outdoor Exploration: Collaboratively venture into the vast wilderness and commence an expedition. Enjoy a picnic or kayaking, or organize a scenic trek in a lovely park. Engaging in outdoor activities facilitates a transformation of the environment and presents a chance to forge lasting connections and exchange novel experiences.

Incorporate culinary pursuits into your date night by enrolling in a cookery class or jointly attending a food festival. Conversely, one could attempt to prepare a novel dish at home or engage in a friendly culinary competition. Collaboratively preparing and savoring a delectable meal can serve as a pleasurable means of strengthening bonds.

Themed Movie Nights: Hodges-themed movie marathons to elevate the movie night experience. Create an inviting home theater environment by selecting a motif, such as classic romance, films from the 1980s, or films from a specific genre. Blankets and refreshments are essential for a romantic movie night at home.

City Scavenger Search: Organize a scavenger search to explore your city enjoyably and interactively. Collaboratively generate a catalog of hints that point to momentous locations or cherished recollections and derive pleasure from resolving them. This introduces an aspect of excitement and enables you to reevaluate your immediate environment.

Live Performances: Embark on an enthralling experience of live entertainment. Attend a live music performance, a comedy show, or a local theater production. Experiencing live performances together can be an incredibly romantic and sophisticated addition to your date evenings.

Observing Getaway: Spend the night observing while escaping the city lights. Engaging in astronomy, whether while camping beneath the stars or simply lounging on a blanket in a secluded area, fosters a serene atmosphere conducive to meaningful conversations and intimate moments of connection.

Virtual Adventures: Embrace virtual date ideas for long-distance relationships or situations with problematic physical proximity. By facilitating online escape rooms and virtual museum excursions, technology can enable individuals to share enjoyable experiences from the convenience of their locations. Developing a solid foundation in the early phases of a new relationship requires shared experiences and moments of happiness. By integrating innovative date concepts into your weekly schedule, you inject enthusiasm into your partnership and amass a wealth of recollections that will strengthen your connection. Therefore, venture out into the unknown and allow the enchantment of creative dating to enhance the connection between you and your significant other.

Transitioning With Me

There must come a time in the dating process when individuals who have mutually chosen to remain together should advance their relationship. This is indeed courtship. Boundaries would be established, and assumptions would be made in this context.

Certain actions of a partner would cause their partner to feel sorrow, whereas an ordinary acquaintance could perform the same deed without eliciting the same response. Implied expectations may include specific forms of conduct.

A woman would expect her pursuer to be exclusively committed to her. While she might express this to the male openly, he is generally expected to be aware of this expectation.

However, there are certain matters that partners expect their partners to be aware of in terms of their expected conduct. When partners consider such matters without explicitly stating them, their partners' partners often absolve themselves of the implied responsibility concerning the expected behavior.

For example, some women expect a specific level of regularity in check-ups; they anticipate you will pay them a visit within a particular range of frequencies. Occasionally, the man would not be provided with a precise range description.

Thus, she may deliberately refrain from expressing herself to maintain the man within the range that she expects him to complete. However, some males may not perceive any duty upon themselves in that respect.

This may cause the woman to experience perplexity and mistrust; she may conclude that her man has no regard for her or is seeing someone else. Because most implied expectations vary from individual to individual, it is currently only possible to make an educated guess as to what an intended expectation entails. Because of this, transparency is crucial, and presumptive thoughts about a partner can be disastrous if additional investigation is not conducted to confirm the thought's evidence.

However, this does not negate that a partner holds numerous presumptive expectations for his or her companion. One significant factor contributing to relationship dissolution is the inability to comprehend such matters.

There are individuals in relationships where the man enters into a romantic agreement with the woman without proposing, expecting that she will be aware of their union. Women often exploit this implication by courting or proposing to another man who expressly states his motive for romantic involvement.

While such behavior is often deliberate, it is prudent for a male to express his intentions to a woman to prevent potentially dangerous situations that are too common in the modern world.

Similarly, numerous untrustworthy men never enter into committed relationships because their only desire is to seduce, serve, and dominate a woman. They believe that by frequently displaying ill-mannered and employing abusive language, they can induce a state of dread and submission in their companions, thereby rendering their women as possessed property.

Implied feelings a man has for a woman he is dating without openly declaring his interest in her, as well as unattractive demeanors that imply subjugation of a lady, are all inappropriate dating behaviors.

Sometimes, implied actions are manipulative and more potent than explicit ones. An example of this would be a woman presenting an act of deceptive submission to imply a request or a man going above and beyond to entice his partner to bed.

There are numerous repercussions in dating, but there is also an upside. It may be utilized to motivate benevolent actions that can fostering an ongoing romantic relationship.

Indeed, this is the skill that romantic partners ought to acquire, not the inverse.

One can suggest the presence of a loving spirit in a romantic relationship by demonstrating additional care and concern during particular moments and circumstances. Similarly, one can suggest the existence of a stoic nature by being the first to forgive when the need arises.

An instance of hatred in a romantic partnership would inevitably breed more hatred, and the same holds for love. Good deeds, when performed, would foster an environment conducive to the continuation of good deeds in the matter; conversely, bad deeds would have the opposite effect.

Relationships tend to progress in the same way that intentional partners tend to take action. One cannot intentionally exploit their companion and anticipate progress in their romantic relationship. Furthermore, it is impossible to make sacrifices for the betterment of your partner to improve circumstances and anticipate a setback in your romantic relationship.

Both individuals in the relationship are accountable for how the relationship progresses. Whether it expands or contracts in duration depends on how you approach the relationship. Therefore, it is imperative to actively strive towards fostering the relationship. This would require you to practice companionship with your date.

Nevertheless, you must recognize that not every considerate and affectionate individual is appropriate for your company, as the two of you may have quite dissimilar pursuits and interests in life. Navigating religious differences with individuals of a different faith can be extremely challenging.

This typically occurs when one partner refuses to accept the other's worldview and method of devotion in exchange for embracing his or her own. You will know what to do if this is clearly stated to you, as it is customary to disclose this information early on in a dating incident. In this situation, the relationship can be severed if neither party is willing to compromise their beliefs or doctrines to embrace an alternative one.

Nonetheless, some individuals would compromise their faith to be indoctrinated into their spouse's religious practices for admirable qualities in a partner. However, such occurrences are uncommon and exacerbate the distress of families whose religious convictions were violated.

However, this partner must believe that by doing so, he or she will ultimately appear happier and is not concealing his or her true mode of faith to win over the partner's affection. In situations of this nature, one religion must be completely embraced, or it must be sacrificed.

Maintain Your Faith to Your Tastes

If you have come to an understanding of your preferences and aversions, then adhere to them. To connect with someone, avoid caving to their viewpoints and simply agree with what they say. That is the behavior of "people-pleasers," not equal companions. Furthermore, neither a man nor a woman of high caliber enjoys the company of an acolyte.

Remain authentic, irrespective of the perceived danger associated with the potential for a disagreement. Mature individuals can handle disagreements with composure, integrity, and regard for the views of others.

The eighth dating tip is to not let others define you.

Nevertheless, this does not imply that you ought to isolate yourself from novel experiences. Always keep in mind the following: attempt something twice. This straightforward mantra will transform your existence. The initial attempt at something can be tainted by expectations, apprehensions, misgivings, and other factors; this is especially true if one enters the experience with the preconceived notion that it will not be enjoyable. However, two attempts at something will yield a reliable, objective opinion. Maintain an open mind toward new experiences at all times, but be explicit that you are doing so. Clarify if you do not enjoy something after attempting it twice.

A woman who is understanding does not require her partner to concur with or question all of her statements and beliefs. Constantly concurring or disagreeing is not the point. It pertains to maintaining one's convictions unaffected by the viewpoints of others. It makes you appear feeble, indecisive, and influenced by others, unlike an individual with a decisive nature. Unshackled by narrow-mindedness or insecurities, genuine strength and confidence consist of endeavoring every challenge. However, it also upholds the value of honesty and speaking one's genuine viewpoint. While agreeing with your partner's preferences is not obligatory, at least attempt everything equally.

Error made by novice number two

The less effort you can put into the relationship in its infancy, the more beneficial it is. Does this imply you are permitted to behave irresponsibly with a green card? To not care the least bit? No. I am referring to that moment at the beginning of a relationship, when everything is still very new, and you take her out for the first time.

You should strive to keep the activities low-key and unremarkable. You would prefer to avoid introducing her to an expensive restaurant or theme park for the first time. Additionally, it is advisable to conserve money whenever possible. When discussing courting, we refer to socializing and allowing the conversation to flow from point A to point B. Instead of dining at an upscale establishment, visit a local pub where cocktails are available for two for one. If you are compelled to dine at a restaurant, how about substituting McDonald's?

The key is to approach courting and socializing casually. Consider it a social gathering with your closest companion. If you were to spend the day with a good friend, you would probably just laze around town. You might visit a few small stores, grab coffee, and perhaps even visit an art gallery.

Instead of spending hours in one location, attempt to visit various places together that day, such as a supermarket, art store, coffee shop, strolling through stores, or cocktail.

This produces the illusion of time. It will feel as though you two have been acquainted for quite some time, which fosters an immense quantity of comfort and rapport. This is crucial; you should strive to generate maximum comfort within a limited period.

"Invest little, and you will fare better." You can steadfastly adhere to this rule, which will not fail you. However, as the weeks pass and you engage in sexual activity with her, the rule will inevitably alter. During the initial weeks, it is acceptable to devote only 20% of your resources, time, and emotional energy to the endeavor. However, that should increase to 50% within two months and 80% within four months. Additionally, everything depends on how sincere you are with her. Continually spending time with her, engaging in sexual activity, and encountering her will inevitably lead to an increase in your emotional investment.

One crucial insight is to gradually allocate emotional energy towards the relationship. The operative phrase is "slowly." At first, attempt to entice her to invest more in the relationship than you do. Perishable as the months pass, you can invest whatever you desire.

Do as many men do if you desire to destroy your relationship with her: spray her with your fireman emotional water until she flees.

The fireman's emotional hose:

Continue purchasing her items.

Compliment her physical appearance.

Accompany her to pricey restaurants.

Inquire about her aspirations.

Pose an abundance of tedious inquiries.

Make every effort to avoid upsetting her.

Arrogance and Confidence

The majority of individuals would concur that confidence is a seductive quality, whereas cockiness is annoying and foolish. Moreover, it is common knowledge that some women would disparage themselves to obtain compliments. That is unattractive regardless of who commits it.

It is unnecessary to express one's lack of attractiveness. It is advisable to defer to her judgment regarding your physical appearance and bear in mind that if she had any disapproval towards you, she probably would not dedicate much of her time to you. If you have the impression that she is not engaged in a sexual relationship, you should inform her of the nature of the relationship. It is not impossible to make an acquaintance who genuinely appreciates your company. Permitting a woman to request that you pay for meals constitutes continuing to pursue her while unaware of her underlying emotions.

On how many occasions have men perceived a woman who had no intention of developing a romantic relationship as having led him astray and used him as a meal ticket? Might this matter be circumvented if the conversation centered on the relationship? I acknowledge that it is both embarrassing and uncomfortable. However, purchasing twenty dinners for a woman and then demanding that she mount your dick in return is not permissible. You owe her nothing simply because you did her a favor, treated her kindly, or purchased her an item. Simply by sending you pictures of her breasts, she does not owe you a ride on the hobby horse or a blowjob simply because you licked her genitalia.

Believing that a woman will grant your request simply because you grant hers is tantamount to adhering to Cosmopolitan guidelines for enticing a submissive man to your service. Your participation in her game will almost undoubtedly alert her that you are doing so.

THAT SHOULD NOT HAPPEN.

Although I've repeatedly stated that you must never make the woman feel like you are playing with her, for the love of God, do not allow yourself to be played by her, either. Men who give in to the machinations of foolish women are not only the source of ignorant advice articles directed at lonely women, but they are also solely responsible for their actions.

Is a woman telling you a lie, or have you simply neglected to inquire? Did she mislead you, or did you interpret "signals" that did not exist? Conversely, the only way to prevent this from occurring to you is to discuss it. She might deceive you and be a vile woman plying from the depths of Satan's abyss, but that is not my call to make; rather, that is yours to decide. Most of the time, you will gain insight into the situation that will dictate your next move if you force yourself through the "relationship talk" and inquire about a woman's desires and aspirations.

Platonism, on her part, indicates that you retain your autonomy. Acknowledging her uncertainty can provide valuable insights into the course of action you should pursue.

When engaging in a discussion, remember that while seeking responses from others, you cannot coerce them. She will divulge her thoughts and feelings if she is at ease. If she appears to be evading the discussion, consider commencing by expressing your emotions. Place oneself in a position of vulnerability. In contrast, you may always provide her with a response. If she appears reticent throughout the conversation, you may inquire whether she is uncertain or perplexed about a particular matter. Simply permitting her to experience uncertainty can be extremely reassuring for her. When dealing with an uncertain woman, it is advisable to provide reassurance and exercise extreme caution when engaging in physical contact until she attains clarity regarding her emotions and expectations.

Women completely lose faith in males when they enter physical or emotional relationships without being able to support their claims with action and commitment. This often occurs in women, complicating matters for males who desire to develop genuine relationships. Obtaining agreement with your companion is the most beneficial action that you can take for yourself. Sexual contact with a woman who is unsure of her emotions may result in your isolation or the woman feeling exploited and wounded. The sensation of being exploited, wounded, and vengeful is what propels women down exceptionally bizarre, "crazy"-paths, in the opinion of the majority. Certain individuals begin to impersonate inadvertent text messages and share explicit images on social media to demonstrate their attractiveness and the extent to which you miss them. Some women even pose to be pregnant or appear at locations you frequent. Avoid the distress and meditate on it in your underwear until you are certain both parties have identical expectations for the interaction.

Chapter Three: Lovers to Friends

It could be more convenient to be in a relationship with someone you have not seen in years rather than with someone with whom you spend most of your free time, socialize, or share humiliating stories.

Patience is a magical word necessary if you are contemplating transforming a friend into a lover. It will require that you proceed with caution. Frequently, expressing your emotions hastily without providing hints may alienate the other individual, preventing you from ever having the opportunity to develop your connection further. It is indeed beneficial to be candid with them regarding your emotions; however, you must also choose the appropriate moment to do so.

However, attempting to transform a friend into a companion could deteriorate the friendship. Therefore, before contemplating expressing your emotions, allocate sufficient time to determine whether they are firmly established. Suppose it is merely physical attraction, or you are unsure about it. In that case, you should carefully consider your emotions on multiple occasions, as they could result in a transient romantic commitment. You may not be willing to sacrifice a good friendship for one.

The opportunity to spend time with a loved one is among the numerous pleasures in life. Therefore, how does one establish such a relationship when they have exhausted all conventional approaches to meeting new individuals without success? It is conceivable that your approach may be flawed.

Many individuals encounter individuals they like and subsequently begin dating them. This model is frequently preoccupied with the superficial, and crucial details are frequently overlooked until much later, resulting in sorrow and suffering.

However, if you reverse that notion, you will arrive at a more refined approach to dating: Prioritize friendships over dating.

This can be accomplished by approaching the person of interest as you would a typical engagement. Engage them in date-like activities and take them to a location other than the typical hangout for peers. Animus them with affection. Ensure that they feel secure and protected in your presence. You may tease them by employing body language you would not ordinarily employ in their presence, such as gently encircling their arms or tickling them while observing their reactions. You can determine whether or not an attraction exists between you in this manner.

Determine the ideal moment to express your emotions to them. Over time, the more you treat them as if they were on a date, the more enjoyable it will be for them. The more they observe how you behave as a companion, the more they encourage them to consider developing feelings for you romantically. You may discover precisely the correct hint to advance the relationship to a higher level in this manner.

It is important to note that in the event of an unsuccessful intimate relationship with a friend, the nature of their friendship will irrevocably change. If you are prepared to compromise this in exchange for the opportunity to express your emotions and at least attempt to resolve the relationship, that would not be so terrible. You will not even be sorry that you did not attempt.

The benefit of transforming an acquaintance into a lover is that you can be completely candid with one another from the beginning of your "dating." You may also discuss the relationship's potential outcomes, such as whether you wish to maintain your friendship if it fails.

Changing acquaintances into romantic partners is likely more difficult than traditional dating. Still, if it succeeds, you may also have a good shot at establishing a relationship that lasts a lifetime.

Do you wish your friend were more than an acquaintance and instead became your lover? Do you feel infatuated with her? Hey! That is certainly feasible, provided you have the necessary knowledge.

www.ingramcontent.com/pod-product-compliance
Lightning Source LLC
Chambersburg PA
CBHW052136110526
44591CB00012B/1744